ALIGNED
A Real Talk Guide To Balancing Mind, Body, And Spirit

Brandie Sophiel

Copyrights © 2025 by Brandie Sophiel

All rights reserved.

Dedication

I dedicate this book to the Divine Universe, for its infinite wisdom and guidance. To my spiritual ancestors, whose presence continues to shape and inspire my path. To my children, Aubri, Lynn, and B.P.; my mum, my dad, and Mama Trish; my siblings; my family; and close friends, Chris, Becka, Parker, and Kendall, whose love and support remind me daily of the power of connection.

To the Divine Presence of stillness and oneness, which teaches us the beauty of living in harmony. And to Nature, for offering your gifts that nourish the body, mind, and spirit.

May we all continue to align with the flow of life, ever grateful for the blessings we receive from the universe.

TABLE OF CONTENTS

Introduction: Let's Keep It Real — 1

Chapter 1: What Alignment Really Means (And Why It's Not About Perfection) — 2
- *What Alignment Really Feels Like* — 3
- *Why Alignment Isn't About Perfection* — 3
- *How to Start Living Aligned with Your Higher Purpose* — 4
- *How to Know When You're Out of Alignment with the Greater Plan* — 5
- *Embracing the Sacred Process of Alignment* — 5
- *Summary:* — 7

Chapter 2: Get Out of Your Head (And Into Your Life) — 8
- *Mind Alignment: Reconnecting with Inner Wisdom* — 9
- *Practice Mindfulness and Meditation* — 9
- *Journal Your Thoughts in Communion with Your Higher Self* — 10
- *Challenge Your Thoughts through Clarity and Discernment* — 10
- *Affirmations, Visualization, and Seeking Guidance* — 11
- *Limit Your Input to Nourish Your Soul* — 11
- *Take Action Guided by Your True Essence* — 12
- *Summary:* — 13

Chapter 3: Your Body Knows What's Up — 14
- *The Sacred Language of Your Body* — 15
- *What Your Body's Trying to Tell You (Messages from Within)* — 15
- *Small Shifts, Big Impact in Divine Alignment* — 16
- *No Guilt, Just Alignment with Your True Self* — 17
- *Summary:* — 18

Chapter 4: Finding Your Flow — 19
- *Finding Your Sacred Connection* — 20
- *Nature as a Portal to Divine Energy* — 21
- *Tapping into Your Spirit, the Temple of Your Soul* — 21
- *Grounding Your Spirit in Trust* — 22

No Pressure, Just Connection with the Flow of Life	22
Summary:	24

Chapter 5 Balance, Not Perfection — 25

It's About Progress, Not Perfection in Your Spiritual Journey — 26
Tools for Staying Aligned with Your True Purpose — 27
Staying Aligned Through Life's Challenges by Trusting the Process — 28
You Are the Constant in the Divine Design — 28
Summary: — 29

Chapter 6: Overcoming Resistance — 30

Why We Resist Alignment — 31
Recognizing Resistance as Spiritual Disconnect — 31
Transforming Resistance into Growth through Clarity and Faith 32
Practical Tools for Overcoming Resistance: — 32
Summary — 33

Chapter 7: Aligning with Your Values — 34

Getting Clear on Your Core Values through Inner Wisdom — 35
Aligning Decisions with Your Higher Purpose — 35
Reevaluating Your Values in the Light of Spiritual Understanding — 36
Summary: — 38

Chapter 8: The Power of Stillness — 39

The Role of Silence and Meditation in Alignment — 40
Practices for Stillness: Meditation, Reflection, and Presence — 40
Letting Go of the Need for Constant Action and Trusting Divine Timing — 42
Summary: — 43

Chapter 9: Alignment in Your Career and Creativity — 44

Living Aligned with Your Sacred Work — 45
Unleashing Creative Potential as a Divine Gift — 45
Practical Steps for Career-Aligned Action Guided by Your Higher Purpose — 46

Summary:	49
Chapter 10: Money and Abundance in Alignment	**50**
Redefining Your Relationship with Money as a Spiritual Resource	51
Creating an Aligned Abundance Mindset through Trust	51
Aligned Financial Decisions: Stewardship and Prosperity in the Flow of Life	52
Practical Steps for Creating an Aligned Relationship with Money:	53
Summary:	54
Chapter 11: Aligning Through Challenges	**56**
Staying Aligned When Life Gets Tough: Leaning into Inner Strength	57
Growth Through Adversity: Spiritual Refining	57
Practical Tools for Resilience: Trust, Reflection, and Strengthening Your Spirit	58
Self-Compassion:	59
Summary:	61
Chapter 12: The Art of Surrender	**62**
Surrendering to the Divine Will for True Alignment	63
Trusting the Process: Walking with Faith	63
The Power of Acceptance: Surrendering to Timing and Flow	64
Summary:	66
Chapter 13: Creating Aligned Habits for Long-Term Success	**67**
Sustaining Alignment Through Daily Devotion and Practice	68
Building Healthy, Aligned Habits in Service to Your True Purpose	68
Tracking and Reflecting on Your Spiritual Progress	69
Summary:	71
Chapter 14: The Role of Gratitude in Alignment	**72**
Gratitude as a Tool for Realigning with Abundant Energy	73
The Science of Gratitude and Spiritual Blessings	73

Cultivating Gratitude in Everyday Life as a Spiritual Practice	74
Summary:	76
Chapter 15: Living Aligned with the Universe	**77**
Trusting Universal Timing and Divine Order	78
Aligning with the Flow of Life's Purpose	78
Signs, Synchronicities, and Divine Guidance	79
Summary:	80
Conclusion: You've Got This	**81**
Key Takeaways:	82
Bonus Chapter: Walking in Alignment Beyond These Pages	**83**
Integrating Alignment into Everyday Life	84
Honoring Your Journey Without Judgment	84
Continuing the Path of Growth, Peace, and Purpose	85
A Sacred Prayer for Alignment	86

Acknowledgments

I would like to express my deepest gratitude to those who have inspired and supported me throughout this journey. A special thank you to Gary, whose encouragement and belief in the power of sharing one's voice inspired me to take the step of writing this book.

To everyone who has been a part of this process, whether through direct support or simply by being a source of inspiration, your impact has been invaluable. Each of you, in your own way, has helped shape the creation of this book, and for that, I am truly grateful.

Introduction: Let's Keep It Real

Alignment is one of those words we hear a lot in spiritual circles, but what does it actually mean? It's not about being perfect or having all the answers—it's about getting in tune with the deeper truth inside you and the flow of the universe around you. It's about understanding that you're part of something much bigger and finding ways to live in harmony with that bigger picture.

Living in alignment isn't some lofty goal you reach after years of perfect practice. It's a journey, a daily choice to show up as your authentic self and trust that you're on the right path, even when things get messy. Whether you call it the divine presence, universal energy, or just the flow of life, it's there, guiding you, if you're open to it.

This book is about helping you reconnect with that presence—your truest self—and learn to navigate life in a way that feels meaningful, grounded, and, most of all, aligned with who you really are. It's about making small shifts that lead to big changes and trusting the process along the way. Because, at the end of the day, when you're aligned with your true purpose, everything else starts to fall into place.

So let's keep it real—no pressure, no expectations—just a commitment to showing up, being honest with ourselves, and letting life unfold in its own beautifully imperfect way.

Chapter 1:
What Alignment Really Means (And Why It's Not About Perfection)

Alignment. It's a buzzword we hear a lot these days, but what does it really mean? At its core, alignment is about being in sync with your true self and the bigger picture of life—whatever that looks like for you. It's that feeling when everything just *clicks*—when your actions, thoughts, and energy are all headed in the same direction. But, here's the thing: alignment is not about getting it all right or being perfect. Far from it. In fact, perfection might just be one of the biggest obstacles to true alignment.

What Alignment Really Feels Like

When you're in alignment, you know it. It feels like flow. It's when you're doing the right things without forcing them, when you feel connected to something greater than yourself, even if it's just in a moment of stillness. It's that deep sense of peace, clarity, and purpose, even in the middle of life's chaos. You feel like you're where you're supposed to be, even if you're not sure exactly where that is. Alignment isn't about having every answer, but rather trusting that you're moving in the right direction, even if it's just one small step at a time.

Alignment also feels like being grounded. You can be in the middle of uncertainty, but somehow you still feel solid in your bones, knowing you're moving with the current of your purpose. It's a quiet kind of confidence, a deep knowing that everything, even the tough parts, is unfolding as it should.

Why Alignment Isn't About Perfection

A lot of us have been sold this idea that to be aligned, we have to be perfect. We've got to have it all together—perfect relationships, perfect career, perfect mindset. But that's not what alignment is. Alignment is messy. It's a process. It's about finding harmony in the mess of life, not avoiding it or trying to perfect it. The truth is, we're human. And being human means we'll make mistakes, get distracted, get off track, and have those days when nothing seems to click.

But guess what? That's all part of the journey. Alignment isn't about perfection; it's about progress. It's about moving in the right direction, even when it feels like you're stumbling. It's about accepting that imperfection is part of the deal and trusting that you'll keep course-correcting along the way. There's no "perfect" version of alignment to achieve, just an ongoing process of checking in with yourself, recalibrating, and finding your way back when you get lost. And getting lost? That's okay. It's how we find ourselves.

How to Start Living Aligned with Your Higher Purpose

So, how do you start living in alignment? It's not some huge, dramatic shift that happens overnight. It's a series of small, conscious choices. It's about tuning in to your inner voice, paying attention to what feels right, and what doesn't. It's about checking in with yourself regularly and asking: "Is this what I truly want?" or "Does this align with my values and my deeper purpose?"

One of the easiest ways to get started is by creating space for self-reflection. That might look like journaling, meditating, or simply sitting with yourself in quiet moments. Start paying attention to what lights you up and what drains you. Notice where you feel connected to something greater than yourself, and where you feel disconnected. Your higher purpose is often found in these small, quiet moments of self-awareness.

Don't try to force it. Alignment isn't something you can force or rush into. It's about making choices that feel true to who you are, even if they're small or imperfect at first. Every step in the right direction counts.

How to Know When You're Out of Alignment with the Greater Plan

So, what happens when you're out of alignment? You feel it. You feel drained, frustrated, or disconnected. Things feel like they're pushing against you rather than flowing. You might start to feel lost or stuck, like you're going through the motions without any real direction or purpose. Maybe you're forcing things that aren't working or staying in situations that don't feel right.

The key is to tune into those signs. When you're out of alignment, there's usually some kind of internal warning system—an uncomfortable feeling, a sense of resistance, or even physical tension in your body. It's like your intuition or your soul trying to tell you, "Hey, something's off here." It's not about perfection—it's about being aware and open to adjusting when something doesn't feel right.

When you notice you're out of alignment, the first step is to slow down. Don't just push through. Take a moment to reflect on what's really going on. Ask yourself what feels off, and why. This process of awareness is the first step in realigning with your higher purpose.

Embracing the Sacred Process of Alignment

Finally, alignment is not a one-time event. It's an ongoing, sacred process. You'll realign again and again, each time getting a little clearer, a little more connected to your true self and your purpose. And that's the beauty of it. Life is a dance, and sometimes you'll be in sync, and sometimes you'll step out of rhythm. But every step, every misstep, is part of the dance.

Embracing this process means giving yourself grace. It means understanding that alignment isn't something to chase or perfect—it's something to experience, moment by moment. It's the ebb and flow of life, learning to be present with yourself in each phase, trusting that you're always being guided, even when you can't see the whole picture.

Summary:

Alignment is about being in tune with your true self and the greater flow of life, not about achieving some ideal of perfection. It's that sense of peace, purpose, and flow that you feel when things click into place. But it's also something that evolves over time, not a one-time achievement. When you find yourself off track, don't see it as a failure—it's simply part of the process. By embracing this journey, you can start making small, intentional shifts toward living more in alignment with your higher purpose. And remember, the real beauty is in the constant realignment, not in a destination.

Chapter 2:
Get Out of Your Head (And Into Your Life)

We've all been there: stuck in our heads, caught up in endless thoughts, overthinking every little detail, and getting overwhelmed by the noise. It's easy to get lost in the mental chatter, but here's the thing—your head isn't always the best place to live. True alignment comes when you reconnect with something deeper, something that feels true and grounded. This chapter is all about how to get out of your head and start living from that deeper place, where your inner wisdom and intuition guide you forward.

Mind Alignment: Reconnecting with Inner Wisdom

Your mind is a tool—one of many in your life—but it's not the only tool you should rely on. We tend to overthink and let our minds take the wheel, but your inner wisdom, your intuition, is often a much better guide. Aligning your mind means quieting the mental noise and tuning into the deeper part of you that already knows what's best. It's about shifting from analysis paralysis to trusting the gut feelings, hunches, and nudges that come from within.

Reconnecting with that wisdom requires getting still and learning how to listen to it, rather than just thinking your way through everything. It's about tapping into the space that exists *beneath* your thoughts, where clarity, peace, and guidance often reside.

Practice Mindfulness and Meditation

Mindfulness and meditation are two powerful tools for aligning your mind. When you're mindful, you're present in the moment, not caught up in the past or worried about the future. It's about noticing the small details of your experience—your breath, the sounds around you, the sensations in your body. This awareness helps you tune into your inner guidance.

Meditation is a great way to strengthen this practice. It doesn't have to be long or complicated—just a few minutes of quiet reflection each day can help quiet the noise and bring you back to center. In meditation, you start to separate yourself from your thoughts. You realize that you are *not* your thoughts, and in that space, your inner wisdom can emerge.

Journal Your Thoughts in Communion with Your Higher Self

Journaling isn't just about writing down what happened during your day. It's a tool for connecting with your higher self, your truest essence. When you journal, you get out of your head and onto the page. It's a way to release all that mental clutter and start connecting with deeper thoughts and insights.

Start with free writing—just letting whatever comes up flow onto the page. You might be surprised at the clarity you find, even in the middle of chaos. Ask yourself questions like, "What's on my mind right now?" or "What do I truly want?" Allow yourself to be open to whatever emerges. The act of writing becomes a conversation with your higher self, a way to receive answers and guidance that might not come through when you're just thinking things over.

Challenge Your Thoughts through Clarity and Discernment

Your mind can sometimes get in its own way, creating stories and narratives that aren't true. We all have that inner critic, the voice that tells us we're not enough or we can't do something. But you don't have to believe everything that pops into your head. This is where clarity and discernment come in.

Start to challenge your thoughts by asking yourself: *Is this true? Is this helpful? Does this align with who I really am or what I really want?* If the thought is based on fear or old stories, let it go. The more you practice this, the easier it gets to discern which thoughts are serving your alignment and which ones are simply distractions.

Being discerning means learning to trust the voice that speaks with clarity and wisdom, not the voice that stirs up anxiety or doubt. You can choose to step back and make space for the more grounded, aligned thoughts to take the lead.

Affirmations, Visualization, and Seeking Guidance

Sometimes our minds need a little extra boost to align with our higher purpose. That's where affirmations and visualization come in. Affirmations are positive statements you repeat to shift your mindset. They help reprogram old, limiting beliefs and replace them with empowering ones. Instead of thinking, "I'm not good enough," try, "I am worthy of success and peace." The more you repeat affirmations, the more you start to believe them.

Visualization is another powerful practice. When you visualize your goals and dreams as if they've already happened, you start to align your mind with the possibility of those things coming into your life. It's like creating a mental blueprint for your future, one that draws your reality closer.

Along with these practices, don't be afraid to seek guidance. Whether it's from a mentor, a spiritual practice, or simply by asking the universe for clarity, seeking guidance helps bring you back to alignment. Sometimes, you just need that nudge to remind you of the bigger picture.

Limit Your Input to Nourish Your Soul

We live in an age of constant information. Social media, news, podcasts, books... there's always something to consume. But not all of it is nourishing for your soul. If you're constantly filling your mind with external input, you may find it harder to hear your inner wisdom. It's easy to get overwhelmed and distracted by all the noise.

To realign your mind, try limiting the amount of input you take in. Set boundaries around your media consumption. Choose what nourishes you—content that makes you feel inspired, grounded, and connected to your true self. And, importantly, create time for silence. The less you fill your mind with outside noise, the more space you create for your own thoughts, insights, and guidance to come through.

Take Action Guided by Your True Essence

Finally, alignment is not just about thinking or feeling—it's about *doing*. Taking action is how you bring your inner wisdom to life. But here's the key: this action has to come from your true essence, not from a place of fear, obligation, or shoulds.

When you're aligned, your actions feel natural and in flow. You don't force things. You take steps that feel right, that are guided by your deeper wisdom, rather than by the demands of your busy mind. When you're in tune with your inner guidance, the steps you take will lead you forward—sometimes in unexpected but beautiful ways.

Summary:

Take a moment to check in with your mind. How often do you feel overwhelmed by distractions or endless thoughts? Finding alignment starts with reconnecting to your true self—slowing down to get clear on what really matters. Practices like mindfulness or journaling help create space for inner wisdom. It's not about perfection, but staying present and open to the process. When you limit the external noise and take action aligned with your true self, clarity follows. Trust your inner compass, show up for yourself, and move with intention.

Chapter 3:
Your Body Knows What's Up

We spend a lot of time in our heads, but our bodies? Our bodies are constantly sending us messages. Every ache, every tension, every burst of energy is a clue, a piece of the puzzle that helps us livae in alignment with who we really are. Our bodies are far more than just vessels that carry us through the day; they are powerful messengers, channels of wisdom that help guide us back to our true essence.

In this chapter, we're going to dive into how to tune in to your body's signals and use that deep, intuitive wisdom to live more fully in alignment.

The Sacred Language of Your Body

Your body speaks in a language of its own. It's not always words or thoughts; often, it's feelings, sensations, and subtle shifts that tell you what's really going on beneath the surface. But just like any language, it's up to you to learn how to listen and interpret these signals.

When we talk about the sacred language of your body, we mean the deeper, intuitive wisdom it holds. Every physical sensation—from a knot in your stomach to a burst of energy in your chest—is a message. But to hear these messages, you have to slow down and become present in your body. Your body is always trying to tell you something, but you've got to stop running on autopilot long enough to listen. The more you tune in, the more you'll hear and understand its wisdom.

What Your Body's Trying to Tell You (Messages from Within)

Your body communicates in ways that can be hard to ignore once you know what to look for. Those tight shoulders? Maybe they're telling you that you're carrying too much stress or holding onto old emotions. The fluttering in your chest? That could be your heart center calling you to follow your passions or step into something new. A feeling of heaviness or lethargy? Your body might be asking you to slow down, rest, and recharge.

Often, we don't listen to these messages, either because we're too busy or because we don't know how to interpret them. But your body is always speaking the truth—it's just that sometimes the truth is uncomfortable or inconvenient. When you feel tension or discomfort, instead of pushing through, try to ask yourself: *What am I really feeling right now? What does my body need from me in this moment?* It might be calling for rest, a shift in your routine, or a deeper emotional release. Trust that your body has the answers—it's been with you through it all, after all.

Small Shifts, Big Impact in Divine Alignment

One of the beautiful things about working with your body's wisdom is that even small changes can have a huge impact on your alignment. You don't have to make dramatic shifts to experience big results. Sometimes it's as simple as adjusting your posture, taking a few deep breaths, or choosing to stretch out the tension that's built up throughout the day. These small acts of self-care are more than just physical—they're acts of alignment.

When you listen to your body and make adjustments, you create space for things to flow more easily. Your energy, emotions, and thoughts align, and that sense of harmony starts to reflect in your outer world. For example, if your body's telling you to slow down and you actually listen by resting or doing something nourishing, you're sending a powerful message to your mind and spirit that you are worthy of care. It's the little shifts in how you treat yourself that bring big shifts in how you feel and how you show up in the world.

Remember, alignment doesn't require perfection. It's about making the small, loving changes that bring you closer to feeling balanced and whole. Start paying attention to the little things your body is asking for, and trust that these small shifts will lead to a bigger, more aligned life.

No Guilt, Just Alignment with Your True Self

One of the biggest barriers to listening to our bodies is guilt. We often feel guilty for taking breaks, for resting, for saying no, or for doing things that feel good but don't always fit into our busy schedules. But guilt has no place in alignment. The truth is, your body needs love and care just as much as your mind and spirit do. When you ignore your body's needs, you start to feel disconnected from your true self. And when you listen to your body with love and attention, you align more deeply with your essence.

So let go of the guilt. It's okay to rest when you need it. It's okay to say no to things that drain your energy. It's okay to prioritize your well-being. You don't have to earn rest, and you don't have to hustle non-stop to prove your worth. Your body is part of your sacred alignment. It's your companion, not something to push aside or ignore. By giving your body the care and respect it deserves, you align more fully with your true self—and that's when everything starts to flow.

Summary:

Your body is a powerful guide to living in alignment. By listening to its messages—whether they're physical sensations or emotional cues—you can make small shifts that lead to big changes in your life. Let go of guilt and listen to your body without judgment, knowing that each loving action you take is part of your divine alignment with your true self.

Chapter 4:
Finding Your Flow

Life can often feel like a series of obstacles or a never-ending to-do list. But there's another way to experience life—one that feels easy, effortless, and in alignment with your true self. That's what we call *finding your flow*. It's about letting go of the struggle and reconnecting with the natural rhythm of life, where everything unfolds with ease, where you're tuned into the sacred energy of the universe, and where you are no longer fighting against the current, but flowing with it.

In this chapter, we'll explore how to reconnect with that divine flow—the energy that moves through everything—and how to trust it. When you're in your flow, you're in alignment with your truest self, and everything just falls into place.

Finding Your Sacred Connection

Finding your flow begins with finding your sacred connection—the invisible thread that ties you to everything in the universe. It's that sense of connection to something bigger than you, something that's been guiding you all along. This connection is unique to you, and it shows up in different ways. For some, it's a sense of peace that arises when you're alone with your thoughts. For others, it's a deep sense of purpose when you're doing something that aligns with your soul's mission.

This connection doesn't have to be loud or dramatic—it can be quiet and subtle, but it's always there. The key is to become aware of it. Pay attention to the moments when you feel most in tune with yourself. What were you doing? Where were you? Who were you with? When you start to recognize these moments, you can intentionally create more space for them, deepening your connection and allowing your life to flow more naturally.

Nature as a Portal to Divine Energy

One of the easiest ways to reconnect with your flow is through nature. The natural world is a powerful portal to divine energy. It's full of life, movement, and rhythm. When you immerse yourself in nature—whether it's a walk through the woods, a hike in the mountains, or simply sitting under a tree—you tap into the sacred energy that moves through all things. Nature has a way of grounding us, reminding us that everything has its own natural rhythm, and we are part of that rhythm.

When you're feeling disconnected or out of sync, nature is one of the best places to find realignment. The trees, the wind, the sun—they're all constant reminders of the flow of life. Let the sounds of birdsong or the feeling of the earth beneath your feet remind you that you, too, are part of this grand cycle of life. Take time to spend in nature regularly, and use it as a tool to reconnect with your sacred connection and realign with your flow.

Tapping into Your Spirit, the Temple of Your Soul

Your spirit is the deepest, truest part of you—the temple of your soul. When you're aligned with your spirit, you're in touch with your highest potential. This part of you knows the way forward, knows what's true, and knows what you're capable of. The key to finding your flow is to tap into this sacred, spiritual aspect of yourself.

The best way to tap into your spirit is by quieting the noise of the mind and simply being present. Meditation, deep breathing, or moments of silence are great ways to create space to connect with your spirit. When you take time to listen to this inner voice, you'll start to feel a sense of ease, knowing that you're guided by a wisdom that transcends everyday concerns.

Remember, your spirit is always there, ready to guide you. It's your connection to the divine, your own inner compass. By tapping into your spirit, you open the door to divine flow.

Grounding Your Spirit in Trust

Trust is a crucial component of flow. You can have all the connection and spiritual awareness in the world, but if you don't trust the process, the flow will be blocked. Trust is what keeps you grounded when things feel uncertain. It's what allows you to let go of control and trust that life is unfolding exactly as it should.

Grounding your spirit means learning to trust the journey, even when it's not clear. It's about knowing that the path you're on is the right one, even if it doesn't look like what you imagined. Grounding is also about bringing your spiritual awareness into your everyday life. Trust that you don't have to have everything figured out; you just have to keep showing up and trusting the process. When you align with trust, you allow the flow of life to guide you.

No Pressure, Just Connection with the Flow of Life

One of the biggest barriers to flow is pressure. We've all felt it—the pressure to succeed, the pressure to "get it right," the pressure to perform at a certain level. But here's the thing: flow doesn't thrive under pressure. It thrives in ease, in connection, and in trust. When you let go of the pressure to have everything figured out, you open up the space to truly connect with the flow of life.

Instead of trying to force things to happen, focus on connecting to the present moment. Breathe. Feel the energy around you. Trust that everything is unfolding as it should. The more you let go of the pressure, the more you'll find yourself naturally flowing with life. Things will fall into place, not because you forced them, but because you allowed them to.

ALIGNED

Summary:

Finding your flow is about reconnecting with your sacred connection, tapping into the energy of nature, and aligning with the deepest part of yourself—your spirit. It's about grounding your spirit in trust and letting go of the pressure to control everything. When you trust the flow of life, everything will align effortlessly, and you'll feel more connected, grounded, and in tune with your true purpose.

Chapter 5
Balance, Not Perfection

In our society, perfection often gets a lot of attention. We see it in social media, in the media, and even in our own expectations of ourselves. But here's the thing: **spiritual alignment isn't about perfection.** It's about balance, growth, and the continual process of becoming the truest version of yourself. This chapter is about embracing the idea that you don't have to be perfect to be aligned—you just need to be real, authentic, and willing to stay in motion.

Balance is the key to maintaining a life of alignment. It's about finding harmony between your mind, body, spirit, and the world around you. Perfection, on the other hand, will always keep you striving for something that can never truly be achieved. Instead, let's focus on progress and how to stay aligned through life's twists and turns, knowing that you're always in the process of unfolding.

It's About Progress, Not Perfection in Your Spiritual Journey

We live in a culture that's obsessed with perfection—perfect looks, perfect relationships, perfect lives—but that ideal is not what spiritual alignment is about. Spiritual growth is a journey, not a destination. It's messy, it's real, and it's constantly evolving. The key is to focus on progress rather than perfection.

When you're aligned with your true purpose, you stop comparing yourself to others and start measuring your success by the small, meaningful steps you take toward becoming the best version of yourself. It's about showing up each day, learning from mistakes, and celebrating the little victories along the way. You might slip, you might stumble, but each step forward counts. It's all part of your divine journey. **Progress** means growth, and growth means alignment with your higher purpose.

So, give yourself permission to be imperfect. When you embrace your imperfections, you actually step into deeper alignment because you're being authentic. There's no need to pretend to have it all together—just focus on moving forward, and the alignment will follow.

Tools for Staying Aligned with Your True Purpose

Staying aligned with your higher purpose is a constant practice, not a one-time event. There are several tools and practices you can rely on to keep you grounded, centered, and aligned, even when life feels chaotic. Some of these tools are internal (mindset, energy, spirit), and others are external (rituals, habits, community). Here are a few key tools to keep in your spiritual toolbox:

1. **Daily Reflection:** Make time each day to check in with yourself. Whether through meditation, journaling, or prayer, create space to reflect on how you're feeling and where you're at in your journey.
2. **Gratitude Practice:** Focusing on what you're grateful for shifts your energy and brings you back into alignment with your higher self. It helps you see the abundance in your life, even when things don't look perfect.
3. **Intuition & Inner Wisdom:** Trust your inner voice. Your intuition will always guide you back to alignment, even when your head tries to overthink things. Practice listening to that quiet, steady voice within.
4. **Sacred Rituals:** Create rituals that help you stay grounded. It could be as simple as lighting a candle, meditating for five minutes, or walking in nature. The point is to create a practice that reminds you of your divine connection.
5. **Community:** Surround yourself with people who encourage and support your journey. Having a like-minded community helps you stay aligned because it provides connection, validation, and shared wisdom.

These tools help you navigate life with a sense of peace, trust, and connection, no matter what challenges you face.

Staying Aligned Through Life's Challenges by Trusting the Process

Let's be real—life isn't always smooth sailing. You'll face obstacles, setbacks, and challenges that can throw you off course. But here's the good news: those challenges are part of the process. They're opportunities to grow, to learn, and to refine your alignment.

When life gets tough, instead of resisting or fighting against what's happening, **trust the process**. Trust that each challenge is here to help you grow stronger, wiser, and more aligned with your true purpose. This doesn't mean you should passively accept everything that comes your way. It means you trust that every twist in the road has a purpose. It's all part of your spiritual evolution.

When you stay aligned through challenges, you recognize that even in difficulty, there's a greater lesson. You learn to trust that life isn't happening to you—it's happening for you. By embracing this mindset, you shift your perspective from victimhood to empowerment, allowing your inner strength and wisdom to guide you through.

You Are the Constant in the Divine Design

Life changes, circumstances shift, and challenges arise, but there's one constant in all of it: **you**. You are the constant, the foundation, the core of your spiritual journey. The external world will continue to change, but when you stay aligned with your true essence, you remain anchored.

You are an integral part of the divine design, and your soul's journey is unfolding exactly as it's meant to. By staying rooted in who you truly are, you become the steady presence that can weather any storm. **Alignment** is not about being in perfect circumstances; it's about being a constant force of truth, love, and presence in the midst of whatever life throws your way.

You don't need external perfection to be aligned. You just need to trust in your ability to stay grounded, present, and authentic, knowing that the divine design is unfolding perfectly, one step at a time.

Summary:

Embracing the journey of spiritual alignment is about progress, not perfection. By using tools like daily reflection, intuition, and sacred rituals, you can stay aligned with your true purpose, even through life's challenges. You are the constant in your divine design—anchored in truth and trust, with the understanding that life is always unfolding as it should.

Chapter 6:
Overcoming Resistance

Why We Resist Alignment

Have you ever found yourself pushing against something you know is good for you? Maybe you felt called to make a change in your life, but something inside you held back. It's a common experience. Resistance often arises when we feel uncertain, afraid, or uncomfortable with the changes that alignment requires. We're creatures of habit, and stepping into the unknown—even if it's for our highest good—can feel daunting.

Resistance is also a protective mechanism. It's our mind's way of keeping us in familiar territory, even if that familiarity no longer serves us. Sometimes, the fear of change or the discomfort of growth can be so intense that we create mental or emotional walls to avoid it. But the reality is, resistance to alignment doesn't protect us; it keeps us from living fully and experiencing the peace, flow, and purpose we're meant for.

Recognizing Resistance as Spiritual Disconnect

It's important to recognize resistance for what it is: a form of spiritual disconnect. When we're out of alignment with our true selves, we feel that tension. It's like trying to fit a square peg into a round hole. You can push, pull, and force it, but it's not going to fit. You may feel stuck, frustrated, or confused, and that's the sign that something deeper is at play.

Resistance shows up in different ways—procrastination, self-doubt, fear of failure, or the constant need to control. These are all signals that we're out of sync with our purpose, our body, or our soul's calling. It's a sign that we're disconnected from the present moment or resisting the flow of life.

When we acknowledge that resistance is not an enemy, but a signal, we can begin to shift our perspective. Instead of seeing it as something to overcome at all costs, we can approach it with curiosity and compassion, understanding that it's simply part of the spiritual process.

Transforming Resistance into Growth through Clarity and Faith

The key to overcoming resistance is clarity and faith. When we can step back and gain clarity on what's truly important to us—what we're really being called to do—it becomes easier to see the resistance for what it is. It's just fear, uncertainty, or old patterns that no longer serve us.

Once we have clarity, faith becomes our anchor. Faith is the trust that the path unfolding before us is for our highest good, even if we can't see the full picture. It's the belief that every step we take in alignment with our truth is leading us to where we need to be.

To transform resistance, we must lean into the discomfort. We don't need to fight it, but we do need to trust that it's part of our growth. Each moment of resistance can be an opportunity to learn something new about ourselves, to grow stronger in our resolve, and to connect deeper with our soul's purpose.

If we stay committed to clarity and trust in the process, resistance will no longer hold us back. It will become fuel for our transformation. What once seemed like an obstacle becomes a stepping stone toward the life we've always wanted—aligned with our true selves, fully connected to our higher purpose.

Practical Tools for Overcoming Resistance:

- **Mindfulness and Awareness**: Start by becoming aware of your resistance. When do you feel blocked or stuck? What thoughts or beliefs come up when you resist change? Simply noticing resistance without judgment can be a powerful first step.

- **Journaling**: Write down your fears, doubts, and the reasons you might be resisting. Seeing them on paper helps you separate yourself from the thoughts and realize they are just passing emotions—temporary and changeable.
- **Breathing and Grounding**: Resistance can create physical tension in the body. Try grounding techniques such as deep breathing, yoga, or walking in nature to reconnect with your inner peace and restore balance.
- **Affirmations and Visualization**: Use positive affirmations and visualization to remind yourself that you are capable of overcoming challenges. Picture yourself moving through the resistance and aligning with your higher purpose.
- **Surrender**: Sometimes, the best way to overcome resistance is to surrender. Let go of the need to control every outcome. Trust the process and know that your soul is guiding you even when you don't have all the answers.

Summary

Resistance is a natural part of the spiritual journey, but it doesn't have to derail you. When you resist alignment, it's often a sign of spiritual disconnect. By recognizing resistance for what it is and transforming it into an opportunity for growth through clarity and faith, you can shift from feeling stuck to stepping into a more aligned and expansive version of yourself. The key is to trust the process and know that every challenge is helping you grow into your truest self.

CHAPTER 7:
ALIGNING WITH YOUR VALUES

Getting Clear on Your Core Values through Inner Wisdom

Our values are the silent forces that guide our choices, shape our behaviors, and define our purpose. They are the deep truths within us that reflect what truly matters. But sometimes, we can get caught up in the noise of daily life or the expectations of others, making it difficult to hear our own inner wisdom. So how do we get clear on what our core values really are?

The process begins with tuning in. It's about connecting with your inner self, going beyond the surface of what you "should" do or what others expect of you. Your values come from the depths of your soul, not from outside influences. To discover them, take time to reflect. Ask yourself:

- What do I hold most dear in my life?
- When have I felt most fulfilled, alive, or aligned?
- What am I willing to stand up for or sacrifice for?
- What qualities do I admire in others and wish to embody?

Journaling can be an incredible tool here. Take a moment to write down what feels truly important to you. Don't worry about getting it perfect; just write from the heart. You might start to notice patterns or themes that reveal your core values—whether it's love, authenticity, creativity, freedom, or something else entirely.

Once you're clear on your values, hold them as a guiding compass. When life gets busy or overwhelming, coming back to your values can help you center yourself, ensuring that you're always making choices that reflect your truest self.

Aligning Decisions with Your Higher Purpose

Once you've identified your core values, the next step is to make sure your daily decisions are in alignment with those values. This is where the magic happens. When you make decisions based on your values, your life begins to flow with greater purpose, clarity, and meaning. But how do you do this consistently?

It starts with checking in with yourself. Before making a big decision—whether it's about your career, relationships, or personal growth—ask yourself: *Does this align with my core values?* If the answer is yes, you'll feel a sense of resonance and peace. If the answer is no, there may be discomfort or resistance. That discomfort is a clue that something is out of alignment.

For example, if one of your core values is integrity, you might find that decisions requiring you to compromise your honesty or principles make you feel unsettled. On the other hand, when you align your decisions with your values—whether it's pursuing a career that speaks to your passions or engaging in relationships that honor your authenticity—you will feel a sense of peace and flow.

Living in alignment with your values means acting with intention and purpose. It's not always easy, and it can require courage, especially when external pressures or temptations pull you in another direction. But remember, your higher purpose is calling you to live authentically, and your values are the map that leads you there.

Reevaluating Your Values in the Light of Spiritual Understanding

As we grow spiritually, we may find that our values evolve. What we once valued deeply may shift as we gain new insights, experience new stages of life, or receive divine guidance. Reevaluating your values isn't about abandoning what once mattered; it's about recognizing how your values evolve in alignment with your spiritual growth.

Sometimes, we might find that certain values we once held—such as success, wealth, or approval from others—no longer hold the same weight as they did before. As you deepen your spiritual practice and understanding, your values may transform into something more expansive and soul-centered.

Take a moment to reflect on your values every so often. Ask yourself:

- Do my current values still serve my highest self?
- Have my experiences or spiritual practice shifted my perspective on what truly matters?
- Am I still honoring my deeper purpose through the choices I make?

This reevaluation process isn't a sign of weakness or indecision—it's a sign of growth. It shows that you're tuning in more deeply to your higher self and allowing your spiritual journey to inform your daily life. Your values are a living, breathing reflection of who you are—and as you evolve, so too do your values.

Summary:

Aligning with your core values is a profound way to live authentically and in tune with your higher purpose. It begins with getting clear on what truly matters to you, making decisions that reflect those values, and periodically reevaluating them as you grow spiritually. When you make choices that honor your values, your life flows with purpose and meaning. Your values are your guiding compass, helping you stay aligned with the divine plan unfolding for you.

Chapter 8:
The Power of Stillness

The Role of Silence and Meditation in Alignment

In a world filled with noise, distractions, and endless activity, it can be hard to hear the whispers of our soul. Yet, silence and meditation hold immense power when it comes to aligning with your true self and divine purpose. These practices create a sacred space within, where you can hear the subtle guidance of your higher self and connect more deeply with the divine flow of life.

Silence, whether in the form of a quiet moment in nature or during a dedicated meditation session, allows your mind to settle and your spirit to speak. The distractions and clutter of daily life fade into the background, making room for inner clarity. In this space of stillness, you begin to tune into what truly matters—your higher purpose, your soul's calling, and the wisdom of the divine presence within you.

Meditation is one of the most effective ways to enter this state of stillness. When you meditate, you intentionally quiet your mind and focus your awareness inward. This practice helps you detach from the constant noise of the world and shift your attention to the deeper rhythms of life. It's in these moments of quiet that alignment becomes clearer, where your connection to your higher purpose strengthens, and where the divine guidance you seek emerges.

By making time for silence and meditation, you open the door to the deeper parts of yourself and invite divine alignment into every aspect of your life.

Practices for Stillness: Meditation, Reflection, and Presence

Stillness is a practice—something that requires intention, patience, and consistency. It's not about forcing yourself into silence but rather allowing yourself the space to *be*. Here are a few ways you can incorporate stillness into your daily life:

1. Meditation:

Meditation is a timeless tool for stillness and spiritual alignment. There are many forms of meditation—some involve focusing on the breath, others involve repeating a mantra, and some are simply about observing your thoughts without attachment. The key is to allow your mind to quiet, creating space for the divine to speak.

Try this: Start with just 5–10 minutes each morning or evening. Sit in a quiet space, close your eyes, and bring your awareness to your breath. If your mind wanders, gently bring it back to the breath or a mantra like "I am aligned." Over time, the more you practice, the deeper your sense of stillness will become.

2. Reflection:

In addition to meditation, reflection is a powerful practice. This can be done through journaling, contemplation, or simply sitting quietly and allowing your thoughts to settle. Reflection is a time to connect the dots in your life, to listen for wisdom from within, and to become more conscious of your inner alignment.

Try this: At the end of each day, reflect on moments where you felt truly aligned, peaceful, or in flow. Journal about these moments and ask yourself how you can bring more of that energy into your life.

3. Presence:

Stillness also arises through presence—the ability to fully engage with the present moment. When you are truly present, you are aligned with the here and now, without worrying about the past or the future. Presence allows you to feel the pulse of life moving through you and helps you trust that you are exactly where you need to be.

Try this: Practice being fully present in whatever you do—whether it's washing dishes, walking in nature, or talking to a friend. Notice how much more aligned you feel when you're truly "there" in the moment.

Letting Go of the Need for Constant Action and Trusting Divine Timing

In a culture that celebrates hustle, productivity, and constant doing, it can be difficult to embrace the power of stillness. We're conditioned to believe that we must always be "doing" in order to be successful or to feel like we're moving forward. But alignment isn't about pushing harder—it's about flowing with the current of life, trusting that the divine plan is unfolding perfectly.

The pressure to always act, always strive, always achieve can be overwhelming. But in the space of stillness, we learn the sacred art of trusting divine timing. Everything unfolds in its own time—when we stop forcing the process and instead allow life to unfold as it's meant to, we step into the flow of divine alignment.

Trusting divine timing means releasing control over the outcome and having faith that what is meant for you will come to you at the perfect moment. It means letting go of impatience and allowing life to move at its own pace, knowing that every step is part of a much larger, divine plan. When you trust in divine timing, you begin to align with the rhythm of the universe, instead of resisting it.

Try this: When you feel anxious about the pace of your progress or uncertain about the timing of events in your life, take a moment to pause and breathe. Remind yourself that you are exactly where you need to be. Trust that the right opportunities, people, and situations will appear when the time is right.

Summary:

The power of stillness lies in its ability to help you align with your higher purpose and divine flow. Silence, meditation, and practices of presence create the space for inner clarity, spiritual connection, and the wisdom of divine timing. When you let go of the pressure to always be "doing" and instead trust that everything is unfolding in its own time, you step into the flow of life with greater ease and alignment. The art of stillness is a powerful tool for spiritual growth—it's in the quiet moments that we hear the deepest truths and find the peace we've been seeking.

Chapter 9:
Alignment in Your Career and Creativity

Living Aligned with Your Sacred Work

Work is not just a job; it's an opportunity to express who we truly are and to serve the greater good. When we align our careers with our higher purpose, work becomes more than a means to earn a living—it becomes an expression of our sacred path.

The key to living aligned with your sacred work is understanding that your job or profession is an extension of your soul's calling. Your work isn't just about what you do—it's about how you show up, the energy you bring, and the impact you make. When you live aligned with your higher purpose, every task you take on feels meaningful and every challenge becomes a stepping stone toward personal and spiritual growth.

Start by asking yourself: *What makes me feel most alive? What are the qualities or talents I have that I want to share with the world?* Your sacred work is often deeply connected to these answers. It's not about finding the "perfect job" in the traditional sense but rather finding a way to serve in a way that feels true to you, whether that's through a career, creative pursuits, or even volunteer work.

When you align your work with your soul's calling, you begin to experience a deep sense of fulfillment that goes beyond external rewards like money or recognition. It's the fulfillment that comes from knowing you are living authentically, contributing to something greater than yourself, and using your unique gifts to make a difference.

Unleashing Creative Potential as a Divine Gift

Creativity isn't just something for artists or musicians—it's a divine gift that resides within every one of us. Creativity is how we express our inner truths, our passions, and our connection to the divine. It's through creativity that we bring our visions to life, whether that's in the form of art, writing, problem-solving, or even the way we approach challenges in our careers and relationships.

The first step in unleashing your creative potential is recognizing that it's already inside of you. You don't need to "find" creativity—it's part of who you are. The divine has gifted each of us with a unique creative spark, and when we nurture it, we allow ourselves to be channels for divine inspiration.

If you've ever felt blocked or disconnected from your creativity, it may be because you've been resisting it or trying to fit into a certain mold. Creativity thrives when it's free to flow without judgment or limitations. It's about stepping outside of the constraints of perfection and allowing yourself to create from a place of joy, curiosity, and playfulness.

In your career, creativity can show up in many forms—whether it's thinking outside the box to solve problems, bringing innovative ideas to the table, or finding new ways to approach your work that feel authentic to you. Your creative potential is a divine gift that can elevate your work, your career, and your life as a whole.

Try this: Start a creative practice—whether it's journaling, sketching, singing, or cooking. It doesn't matter what you create; what matters is that you give yourself permission to play and express without expectation or judgment. Let the act of creation become a form of spiritual connection.

Practical Steps for Career-Aligned Action Guided by Your Higher Purpose

Bringing alignment into your career and creative pursuits doesn't mean everything will magically fall into place overnight. It takes intentional action and consistent steps to move closer to your true calling. Here are a few practical steps you can take to align your career with your higher purpose:

1. Clarify Your Higher Purpose:

The first step is to get clear about what your higher purpose is. This isn't always a straightforward answer, but it's important to ask yourself: *What do I feel deeply called to do? What kind of impact do I want to make in the world?* Take time to reflect on your passions, your natural gifts, and how you can serve others through your work. This clarity will guide your next steps.

2. Set Intentions for Alignment:

Intentions are powerful. Set clear, heart-centered intentions for how you want to show up in your career. This could be as simple as saying, *I am open to living my sacred work, and I trust that the right opportunities will unfold.* Make sure your intentions align with your values, your gifts, and your higher purpose.

3. Take Inspired Action:

It's not enough to just dream about your career alignment—you have to take action! Start by looking for small ways to integrate your higher purpose into your current work. Maybe it's taking on a project that excites you, offering a new service, or simply approaching your work with a renewed sense of purpose. Trust your intuition to guide your steps.

4. Let Go of Fear and Doubt:

Fear and doubt are natural parts of the human experience, but they don't have to hold you back from aligning with your true path. When you feel fear or resistance, recognize it as a sign that you're stepping out of your comfort zone, which is often where the greatest growth happens. Trust that you are supported by the divine and that everything you need will be provided.

5. Stay Open to Divine Opportunities:

Alignment doesn't always happen in the way we expect. Sometimes, the divine has other plans for us that are far greater than we can imagine. Stay open to unexpected opportunities and trust that if something isn't meant for you, something even more aligned will come along.

6. Commit to Ongoing Growth and Learning:

Your career and creative journey will evolve over time. Stay committed to personal and professional growth, always looking for ways to deepen your knowledge, expand your skills, and align more fully with your purpose. This can involve taking courses, seeking mentorship, or simply remaining open to new experiences.

Summary:

Aligning your career with your higher purpose isn't just about finding the right job—it's about connecting with your soul's calling and living that truth through your work. When you view your career as sacred and your creativity as a divine gift, you begin to bring more of your authentic self into everything you do. By clarifying your purpose, setting aligned intentions, and taking inspired action, you can create a career that feels fulfilling, meaningful, and in perfect harmony with your higher self.

Chapter 10:
Money and Abundance in Alignment

Redefining Your Relationship with Money as a Spiritual Resource

Many of us grow up with complex relationships to money—often seeing it as a source of stress, worry, or even guilt. In spiritual circles, money can sometimes be viewed as "dirty" or something that distracts us from our higher purpose. But the truth is, money itself is neither good nor bad. It's a tool, a resource, and when we align it with our higher purpose, it can become a powerful means for creating abundance and serving the world.

In order to live in alignment with abundance, it's crucial to redefine your relationship with money. Think of money not as something to hoard or fear, but as a spiritual resource that can be used for good. When we see money through this lens, it shifts from being a source of tension or limitation to becoming a means of supporting our sacred work, our passions, and our desire to make a positive impact.

By viewing money as a tool for spiritual growth and service, we can begin to understand how it supports our well-being, the well-being of others, and the divine plan at work in our lives. This shift in perspective allows us to feel more abundant, empowered, and aligned with the flow of life.

Try this: Reflect on your current beliefs about money. What messages did you receive about money growing up? How do you feel about wealth and abundance now? Ask yourself how you can begin to see money as a resource that helps you live more fully in alignment with your true purpose.

Creating an Aligned Abundance Mindset through Trust

An aligned abundance mindset is all about trusting that the universe is abundant and that there's always enough for everyone, including you. When you step into trust and believe that abundance is your natural state, you open yourself up to receive what is rightfully yours.

An abundance mindset isn't just about financial wealth—it's about recognizing the abundance in all areas of your life: love, health, creativity, opportunities, and support. When you align with abundance, you begin to see the richness of life in all its forms, and money becomes one of many ways in which you experience and share this abundance.

The key to creating an abundance mindset is trust. Trust that you are worthy of abundance, trust that the universe has your back, and trust that when you are aligned with your higher purpose, everything you need will be provided for you in divine timing. This trust allows you to release the fear and scarcity that often cloud our financial decisions and replace them with faith that everything is unfolding as it should.

Try this: Practice affirmations and visualization to reinforce an abundance mindset. Repeat affirmations like, *I am worthy of abundance, Money flows to me effortlessly,* or *The universe supports my divine purpose.* Visualize yourself living in abundance, feeling secure and at ease with the flow of money in your life.

Aligned Financial Decisions: Stewardship and Prosperity in the Flow of Life

When you make financial decisions from a place of alignment, you move beyond surface-level concerns about bills, debts, or the need to "keep up with the Joneses." Instead, you begin to see money as part of a larger, spiritual flow—a circulation of energy that supports your life purpose and the greater good.

Making aligned financial decisions means asking yourself not just *what will benefit me right now* but *what will best support my higher purpose?* It's about balancing stewardship and prosperity, making wise and thoughtful decisions about how you earn, spend, save, and invest, while always considering how your money aligns with your values and purpose.

One of the most important aspects of aligned financial decisions is stewardship—being responsible with what you've been given and using it in ways that reflect your highest values. This might mean budgeting consciously, choosing where to spend your money based on what truly supports your soul's path, and giving generously to causes or people that align with your spiritual beliefs.

Prosperity doesn't only refer to accumulating wealth—it's about living in harmony with abundance and creating a flow that supports both you and others. Prosperity in alignment means feeling abundant in all areas of your life, not just financially, and making decisions that reflect your soul's calling and greater mission.

Practical Steps for Creating an Aligned Relationship with Money:

1. Release Limiting Beliefs About Money: *

The first step in aligning with abundance is letting go of any limiting beliefs you have about money. These beliefs might sound like, *I don't deserve wealth, Money is evil,* or *There's never enough to go around.* Acknowledge these thoughts and replace them with beliefs that reflect abundance and trust, such as, *I am worthy of wealth, Money is a tool for good,* and *The universe is abundant and supports me.*

2. Create a Financial Vision:

Just like you would create a vision for your career or creative endeavors, create a vision for your financial life. What does abundance look like for you? How much money do you need to feel secure, supported, and free to follow your purpose? Write down your financial goals and set intentions for how money can help you live in alignment with your spiritual mission.

3. Budget with Intention:

Creating a budget isn't just about tracking expenses; it's about aligning your spending with your values. Consider how your money supports your lifestyle and mission. Does your budget reflect your priorities, such as health, self-care, or contributing to the greater good? Be intentional about where your money goes.

4. Practice Gratitude for Money:

Gratitude is a powerful way to align with abundance. When you appreciate the money you have, you open the door for more abundance to flow into your life. Take time each day to be grateful for the resources you currently have, whether it's your income, savings, or the value you receive from spending money. Gratitude shifts your mindset from scarcity to abundance.

5. Generosity and Giving:

A key principle of alignment with money is understanding the flow of giving and receiving. As you align your finances, make sure to contribute to causes or people that align with your values and beliefs. This doesn't always mean large donations; even small acts of generosity can create a powerful flow of abundance. Giving freely aligns you with the greater energy of prosperity.

Summary:

Money, when viewed as a spiritual resource, becomes a tool for personal and collective growth. By redefining your relationship with money, embracing an abundance mindset, and making aligned financial decisions, you move into a space of prosperity where you can live authentically and fulfill your divine purpose. Money is not

ALIGNED

the enemy; it is a channel for alignment with the flow of life—supporting your mission, your well-being, and the well-being of others.

Chapter 11: Aligning Through Challenges

Staying Aligned When Life Gets Tough: Leaning into Inner Strength

When life throws challenges our way—whether it's a personal loss, health struggles, financial difficulties, or emotional turmoil—it's easy to feel disconnected from our higher purpose. In those moments, it can be hard to maintain the sense of alignment that felt so clear when life was flowing smoothly.

The first step in staying aligned during tough times is to lean into your inner strength. This strength is the unwavering sense of self that comes from knowing who you are at a soul level. It's the strength that connects you to something greater than yourself, whether you call it God, the Universe, Source, or your Higher Self. This inner strength is always there, even when you can't feel it.

When challenges arise, take a moment to reconnect with your breath, your body, and your spirit. Ask yourself, *What is this experience teaching me? What is the greater lesson in this challenge?* Reframing challenges as opportunities for growth helps you stay aligned, even when everything feels uncertain.

Try this: When you're facing a difficult situation, practice grounding yourself by taking a few deep breaths and reflecting on your inner strength. You can say an affirmation like, *I am resilient, and I trust that this challenge is guiding me toward greater growth.* Visualize yourself standing firm and centered, no matter what the storm is around you.

Growth Through Adversity: Spiritual Refining

Adversity is one of the most powerful catalysts for spiritual growth. In fact, it's often through our struggles that we are refined, just like gold is purified in fire. These tough times force us to confront our deepest fears, release old patterns, and ultimately become more aligned with our true essence.

When we're going through hardship, we often resist the discomfort. But resistance only prolongs the pain. Instead, allow yourself to feel the pain, but don't let it define you. Adversity can help us strip away ego, unhealthy attachments, and illusions about who we think we are. It's in these moments of darkness that we are most likely to find the light of our true selves.

Think of it like a sculptor chiseling away at a block of stone to reveal the masterpiece hidden inside. You, too, are being shaped and refined through your experiences. Each challenge is a chance to release old beliefs that no longer serve you, make space for new wisdom, and align more deeply with your soul's purpose.

Try this: Reflect on a difficult situation in your life. How did it shape you into who you are today? What lessons did it teach you? Write down any ways you've grown through adversity. This exercise will help you see how challenges contribute to your spiritual refinement.

Practical Tools for Resilience: Trust, Reflection, and Strengthening Your Spirit

Staying aligned during tough times requires tools that can help you build and maintain resilience. Below are a few powerful practices you can use to keep your spirit strong and stay on your path of alignment, no matter what challenges you face.

1. Trust:

Trust is essential when navigating through adversity. Trust that the universe is guiding you, even when the path is unclear. Trust that every challenge has a purpose, and that you are supported on your journey. Trust that this, too, shall pass, and that you will emerge stronger and wiser on the other side.

Try this: Each day, take a moment to reaffirm your trust in the universe. Say to yourself, I trust the divine plan for my life, and I know that I am supported through every challenge.

2. Reflection:

Reflection is a powerful tool for finding meaning in difficult situations. When we reflect, we can see patterns, lessons, and growth that might otherwise go unnoticed. Reflection also helps us process emotions, release them, and move forward with clarity.

Try this: After facing a challenge, take time to journal about the experience. What did you learn from it? How did it help you grow? What strengths did you discover within yourself? Reflecting on these questions helps you find peace and alignment during difficult times.

3. Strengthening Your Spirit:

When you're going through hard times, it's important to nourish your spirit. This may look different for everyone, but strengthening your spirit might involve prayer, meditation, spending time in nature, or connecting with loved ones. The goal is to engage in practices that help you reconnect with your higher self and restore your inner peace.

Try this: Create a daily spiritual practice that helps you stay grounded and aligned. Whether it's a morning meditation, an evening gratitude practice, or weekly nature walks, make space for regular practices that keep your spirit strong and centered. Consistent spiritual nourishment is key to resilience.

Self-Compassion:

Often, when we face challenges, we are our own harshest critics. We may feel like we "should" be stronger, more resilient, or more in control. But self-compassion is essential for maintaining alignment. Give yourself grace when things get tough. Remember that you're human, and it's okay to feel vulnerable. Be kind to yourself as you navigate through challenging times.

Try this: The next time you face a setback or a challenge, practice self-compassion by saying, *I am doing the best I can, and I trust that this is part of my growth.* Remind yourself that it's okay to not have all the answers right away.

Summary:

Aligning through challenges is not about avoiding difficulty, but about using those challenges as opportunities to deepen your connection to your higher self. By trusting in the process, reflecting on your experiences, and strengthening your spirit through self-compassion and spiritual practices, you can navigate life's tough times with resilience. Remember, each challenge is refining you, helping you grow, and aligning you more closely with your true purpose.

Chapter 12:
The Art of Surrender

Surrendering to the Divine Will for True Alignment

Surrender can often feel like a scary word. It might sound passive or even like giving up, but in truth, surrendering is one of the most powerful acts of trust and alignment you can make in your spiritual journey. It's the recognition that there is a divine force at work that knows what's best for you, even when you can't see it yourself.

Surrendering to the divine will means stepping back and allowing life to unfold as it's meant to, instead of constantly trying to control every situation. When we let go of the illusion that we can or should control everything, we make space for divine wisdom to guide us. This doesn't mean we don't take action—it means we take aligned, inspired action instead of pushing or forcing our way forward.

When you surrender to the divine will, you trust that you are being guided to exactly where you need to be. Even if you don't understand the "why" of a situation, surrendering means trusting that there is a higher purpose behind everything you're experiencing. It's the recognition that the universe, or divine presence, is always working in your favor, even when it seems like things are not going according to plan.

Try this: The next time you feel overwhelmed or stuck, practice releasing control. Close your eyes, take a few deep breaths, and say to yourself, *I surrender to the divine will, trusting that I am being guided toward my highest good.* Feel the weight of trying to control slip away as you connect with the peace of surrender.

Trusting the Process: Walking with Faith

Trusting the process is about knowing that every step of your journey is part of a greater plan, even if that plan isn't clear to you in the moment. It's about walking with faith, even when the road ahead feels uncertain or unclear.

Faith doesn't mean having all the answers. It doesn't mean that everything will always be smooth. In fact, trusting the process often means stepping into the unknown with confidence that the next step will reveal itself when the time is right. It's about believing that the universe has your back, and that you are exactly where you need to be, even if it doesn't look like what you expected.

When you trust the process, you stop needing to have everything figured out right away. You learn to be present with what is, to accept where you are, and to move forward in faith that everything is unfolding for your highest good. This faith is a deep knowing that things are happening for you, not to you—and that each experience, no matter how challenging, is part of your divine evolution.

Try this: When you feel the urge to control or over-plan, pause and ask yourself, *Can I trust the process here?* Sit with the question for a moment and allow any anxieties or doubts to release. Simply breathe and remember that you are being guided, step by step.

The Power of Acceptance: Surrendering to Timing and Flow

One of the most powerful aspects of surrender is the ability to accept divine timing and the natural flow of life. We often find ourselves pushing against life's timing, thinking that things should happen *now* or in a certain way. But the truth is, divine timing doesn't operate on our schedule—it operates on the higher wisdom of the universe.

Surrendering to timing means trusting that what is meant for you will come at the perfect time. It's about letting go of the rush and allowing life to unfold organically. When you surrender to the flow of life, you begin to align with the rhythm of the universe. You stop fighting against the current, and instead, you allow yourself to be carried by it, knowing that it will take you where you need to go.

This acceptance can be especially difficult when we're facing delays, setbacks, or things not unfolding as quickly as we'd like. But the power of acceptance is in trusting that the timing of your life is always perfect—even when it doesn't match your timeline. Surrendering to timing helps to relieve frustration, anxiety, and the need for constant control.

Try this: If you're feeling anxious about timing or wanting things to move faster, take a moment to surrender. Close your eyes, take a deep breath, and repeat the affirmation: *I trust that everything is unfolding in divine timing. I accept the flow of life as it is.* Feel yourself release the pressure of trying to control the pace, and allow yourself to relax into the natural rhythm of life.

Summary:

The art of surrender is not about giving up control, but about releasing the need to force outcomes and trusting that the universe is guiding you toward exactly where you need to be. By surrendering to the divine will, trusting the process, and accepting the flow of timing, you align with the higher plan for your life. In surrender, you find peace, freedom, and the wisdom to move forward with faith, knowing that everything is unfolding for your greatest good.

Chapter 13:
Creating Aligned Habits for Long-Term Success

Sustaining Alignment Through Daily Devotion and Practice

Alignment isn't a one-time event—it's a continuous practice. Just as we eat and sleep daily to nourish our bodies, we must also nourish our spirit through daily devotion. Sustaining alignment requires consistent effort, but this effort comes from a place of love and connection, not obligation.

Daily devotion doesn't need to look the same for everyone. For some, it might involve prayer, meditation, or reading spiritual texts. For others, it may include mindfulness practices, gratitude rituals, or even connecting with nature. The key is finding what resonates with you and committing to it regularly.

When we make daily devotion a priority, we create a deep, consistent connection with our higher self. It's like planting seeds of alignment that will grow into a more grounded and peaceful life. The beauty of daily devotion is that it doesn't have to be overwhelming. It can be as simple as setting aside five minutes each morning to connect with yourself, express gratitude, or set intentions for the day.

Try this: Begin your day with a simple ritual that connects you to your higher self. This might be a short meditation, a prayer, or even just sitting quietly and setting an intention for the day. Over time, this small practice will help you stay aligned and focused on your purpose, no matter what comes your way.

Building Healthy, Aligned Habits in Service to Your True Purpose

Creating aligned habits goes beyond just spiritual practices—it involves every aspect of your life, from how you eat and sleep to how you interact with others and how you spend your time. Aligned habits support your true purpose and help you live in harmony with your higher self.

When you align your habits with your purpose, you're creating a life that reflects who you are at your core. For example, if your purpose is to inspire others, you might create habits around sharing your knowledge, being present for others, or engaging in activities that help you grow and develop your gifts. If your purpose involves healing or nurturing others, your habits might center around self-care, learning, and practicing compassion.

The key to building aligned habits is consistency. It's not about doing everything perfectly, but about making small, intentional choices each day that honor your highest good. This might mean choosing to eat nourishing foods, setting boundaries to protect your energy, or spending time doing work that feels meaningful to you.

Try this: Identify one or two habits that you feel are most important for aligning with your higher purpose. These could be habits related to your physical health, emotional well-being, spiritual growth, or how you show up in the world. Write them down and commit to taking small steps each day to build these habits.

Tracking and Reflecting on Your Spiritual Progress

Alignment is a journey, and just like any journey, it's important to reflect on your progress along the way. Tracking your spiritual growth helps you stay connected to your purpose and recognize the shifts and growth you've experienced.

Reflection doesn't have to be a lengthy process. It can be as simple as taking a few minutes each week or month to review how far you've come, what challenges you've faced, and what lessons you've learned. Tracking your progress allows you to celebrate your successes, acknowledge areas for improvement, and refine your practices to stay on track.

One powerful way to track your spiritual progress is through journaling. Write down moments of insight, gratitude, and growth. Reflect on what practices have been most effective in helping you stay aligned, and adjust your habits as needed.

Try this: Set aside time each week to reflect on your spiritual journey. Ask yourself questions like, How did I feel this week in terms of alignment? What habits helped me stay connected to my higher purpose? What challenges did I face, and how did I handle them? This reflection process helps you stay on course and celebrate your progress.

Summary:

Creating aligned habits is about building consistent practices that nurture your mind, body, and spirit. By committing to daily devotion, developing habits that support your true purpose, and reflecting on your spiritual progress, you lay a strong foundation for long-term success in alignment with your higher self. It's not about perfection, but about consistency, intention, and growth.

Chapter 14:
The Role of Gratitude in Alignment

Gratitude as a Tool for Realigning with Abundant Energy

Gratitude is one of the most powerful tools for realigning your energy. When you focus on gratitude, you shift your attention from what's missing or lacking to what's already abundant in your life. This simple shift in perspective can drastically change the way you feel, think, and interact with the world around you.

At its core, gratitude is a practice of appreciation, and appreciation is a magnet for abundance. The more you acknowledge the blessings, big and small, the more you open yourself up to receiving even more. Gratitude aligns you with the energy of abundance, helping you tap into the flow of prosperity, love, and positivity that is always available to you. It realigns your focus on the present moment, which is where the most powerful energy exists.

When you practice gratitude, you start to notice how much you already have—your health, your relationships, your talents, and even the simple joys of life. By acknowledging these blessings, you raise your vibration and align yourself with the abundant flow of the universe. It's like tuning your spiritual radio to the frequency of abundance.

Try this: Begin or end each day by writing down three things you're grateful for. These can be big or small—anything that brings you joy or peace. As you write, focus on how each blessing makes you feel, and allow that feeling of gratitude to fill your heart and mind.

The Science of Gratitude and Spiritual Blessings

Gratitude is more than just a feel-good practice—it has tangible benefits for your body, mind, and spirit. Research has shown that practicing gratitude can boost your mood, improve your physical health, enhance relationships, and even increase your overall life satisfaction. But beyond the science, gratitude has deep spiritual significance.

From a scientific standpoint, gratitude activates the brain's reward centers, releasing dopamine and serotonin—chemicals that promote feelings of happiness, relaxation, and well-being. This is why you feel uplifted and energized when you practice gratitude. On a deeper level, gratitude is a form of spiritual alignment, as it helps you connect with the source of all blessings. It's an acknowledgment that everything you have is a gift, and this perspective naturally opens you to more spiritual blessings.

In many spiritual traditions, gratitude is seen as a direct link to divine favor. When you express gratitude for what you have, you show the universe (or the divine) that you're ready to receive more. It's a recognition of the abundance that surrounds you, which naturally invites more of that energy into your life. Gratitude shifts your frequency to one of appreciation, helping you resonate with the divine and align with your higher purpose.

Try this: In moments of challenge or struggle, take a moment to pause and list things you are grateful for. Even in difficult situations, there is always something to appreciate—whether it's your inner strength, the support of others, or the lesson you're learning. This practice shifts your energy and helps you realign with spiritual blessings.

Cultivating Gratitude in Everyday Life as a Spiritual Practice

While it's easy to be grateful when things are going well, true spiritual alignment comes when you cultivate gratitude in all circumstances. Gratitude is most powerful when it becomes a daily practice—a lens through which you view your life, regardless of external conditions.

Start by bringing gratitude into your everyday moments. The first step is to shift your focus to the present. Rather than dwelling on what you lack or what went wrong, choose to focus on what's already here and now. Whether it's the warmth of your bed in the morning, the smile of a loved one, the beauty of nature, or the simple ability to breathe, these are all blessings to be grateful for.

Gratitude also involves shifting your perspective on challenges. Instead of seeing obstacles as problems, view them as opportunities for growth. In every challenge, there is a lesson, and in every lesson, there is a gift. Cultivating this mindset can completely transform the way you approach life, helping you stay aligned even when things aren't perfect.

As you go about your day, make it a habit to pause and express gratitude for whatever is around you. This can be done silently in your mind or by saying a prayer or affirmation of thanks. By turning gratitude into a daily practice, you naturally align with the energy of abundance and divine flow.

Try this: Throughout the day, practice "gratitude pauses." Set a timer or just notice moments when you can stop and appreciate something around you—whether it's a beautiful moment in nature, a kind interaction with someone, or simply the fact that you're alive and breathing. Each pause of gratitude helps you realign with abundance and the divine.

Summary:

Gratitude is a powerful and transformative practice that can realign your energy with the abundance of the universe. By cultivating gratitude in your daily life, you shift your focus from lack to abundance, inviting more blessings into your experience. Whether through journaling, affirmations, or simply taking time to appreciate the present moment, gratitude helps you stay aligned with your higher purpose and strengthens your spiritual connection. It's a practice that not only enhances your well-being but also aligns you with the divine flow of life.

Chapter 15:
Living Aligned with the Universe

Trusting Universal Timing and Divine Order

When we talk about "universal timing," we're referring to the belief that the universe operates on a rhythm that is perfectly timed for each of us. It's easy to feel impatient when things aren't unfolding as quickly as we'd like, but living in alignment with the universe requires a deep trust in its divine order.

You might have heard the saying, "Everything happens for a reason." This is the core of trusting universal timing: recognizing that there is a perfect timing for all things, even if we don't always see it. Sometimes, what we desire hasn't manifested yet because there's more preparation to be done—whether it's in our hearts, our minds, or our environment. Other times, what we want might not be what we need right now. Trusting the universe means accepting that it's always working in your favor, even if things don't unfold exactly as you expect.

Universal timing isn't about forcing things or rushing the process. It's about having faith that everything will come at the perfect time. The universe is constantly conspiring for your highest good, and when you align with this truth, you allow things to unfold naturally, without resistance.

Try this: Whenever you feel impatience or frustration with the timing of your life, take a deep breath and remind yourself, "I trust that everything is unfolding in divine order." Feel the weight of this trust and allow it to soothe your mind and heart.

Aligning with the Flow of Life's Purpose

Living aligned with your life's purpose isn't about trying to force things into place or chase external validation. Instead, it's about aligning with the flow of your soul's true calling. When you're in alignment, everything feels more effortless, and you experience a sense of flow, where life seems to move with you rather than against you.

To align with the flow of your life's purpose, you first need to connect with your deeper self—your intuition, your heart's desires, and your spiritual guidance. Once you're clear on your purpose, living in alignment means allowing your actions, decisions, and choices to reflect that clarity. It's not about striving—it's about allowing the right opportunities to come your way and trusting that you're always where you need to be.

Alignment with life's purpose also requires letting go of the need to control every aspect of your journey. When you're aligned, you trust that even if things seem uncertain or unclear, there's a greater plan at work. Life's purpose is not always a straight line—it's often filled with unexpected twists and turns, but that's part of the magic.

Try this: Set an intention each day to align your thoughts, actions, and energy with your higher purpose. This could be as simple as asking yourself, "How can I show up today in a way that aligns with my true self?" Take steps, even small ones, in alignment with your soul's calling, and let the universe handle the timing and the outcome.

Signs, Synchronicities, and Divine Guidance

One of the most magical aspects of living aligned with the universe is recognizing the signs, synchronicities, and divine guidance that show up along the way. These moments often feel like little nudges from the universe, gently guiding you in the right direction.

Signs can come in many forms: a random conversation with a stranger, a meaningful song on the radio, or even a dream that feels especially significant. Synchronicities are the seemingly "coincidental" events that occur at just the right time, offering a sense of confirmation that you're on the right path. Divine guidance can appear as intuitive hunches, a feeling of deep knowing, or a sudden shift in perspective that leads to a breakthrough.

When you're living in alignment with the universe, you begin to notice these signs more clearly because your awareness is heightened. The more you pay attention to the little nudges the universe gives you, the more you'll start to notice the big shifts that occur. You begin to trust that these signs and synchronicities aren't just coincidences—they're divine guidance, leading you toward your higher purpose.

Try this: When you experience a synchronicity or a sign, pause for a moment and express gratitude for it. Acknowledge that the universe is guiding you. You can say something like, "Thank you, Universe, for this reminder that I'm on the right path." By acknowledging these moments, you invite more divine guidance into your life.

Summary:

Living aligned with the universe is all about trusting in divine timing, following the flow of your soul's purpose, and being open to the signs and synchronicities that guide you along the way. When you surrender control and trust the process, you align with the greater plan for your life. The universe is always offering guidance, and by staying attuned to it, you can walk through life with confidence, knowing that you're always exactly where you're meant to be. Aligning with the universe brings a sense of peace, purpose, and magic into your life, as you flow effortlessly into your true path.

Conclusion: You've Got This

As we come to the close of this journey, I want to remind you of something incredibly important: *You've got this.* The path of alignment is not about being perfect or having it all figured out—it's about trusting the process, embracing your uniqueness, and knowing deep in your soul that you are exactly where you need to be.

Throughout this book, we've explored how to live in alignment with your higher purpose, how to trust in divine timing, how to overcome resistance, and how to make choices that reflect your true self. All of these teachings are meant to empower you to step into your highest potential. But remember, this is not a destination—it's an ongoing process. Alignment is a journey, one that you will continue to walk for the rest of your life.

You are always aligned with your true purpose, even when it feels like things aren't going the way you want them to. The universe has a greater plan for you, one that's unfolding with every step you take. Even when challenges arise, they are not signs that you've fallen out of alignment—they are opportunities for growth, for refining your spirit, and for deepening your connection to the divine.

Trusting that you are aligned with your true purpose and the universal plan means that you no longer have to force things to happen. It means letting go of the need to control every outcome and instead trusting that the universe is working with you. You can trust that when you follow the path of your soul's calling, you are always in alignment with the highest good, even if it's not always clear at the moment.

Key Takeaways:

- **You are exactly where you need to be**: Whether things are smooth or challenging, know that you are aligned with your divine path. The universe is always guiding you toward what's best for you, even if it doesn't always feel that way.
- **Alignment is a process, not a destination**: There is no "final" point where you've achieved perfect alignment. Every day is an opportunity to realign, to trust, and to grow. Embrace the journey as it comes.
- **Trust the timing of your life**: It can be easy to feel frustrated when things don't unfold the way you want. But remember, the universe's timing is always perfect, and every delay or detour is part of the greater plan.
- **You are supported**: The divine presence is always with you, guiding and nurturing you. Even in moments of doubt or uncertainty, know that you are never alone.

So, as you close this book, take a moment to acknowledge how far you've come on your journey of alignment. You've already taken the first steps by opening your heart and mind to the possibility of living a life that is truly aligned with your purpose. Keep trusting, keep growing, and know that you are always supported in your path.

You've got this. And the universe is right there with you, every step of the way

Bonus Chapter: Walking in Alignment Beyond These Pages

Alignment isn't just something you do in a meditation session or read about in a book. It's a way of living, a way of showing up in the world every day with purpose and intention. This chapter is a reminder that alignment doesn't stop here—it's something that carries on long after you've turned the last page.

Integrating Alignment into Everyday Life

Living in alignment is all about bringing the peace, clarity, and purpose you've been working on into everything you do. It's in the little moments, like making decisions, interacting with people, or even taking a few breaths throughout your day. It's easy to forget, but every moment is an opportunity to reconnect with yourself.

When you're at a crossroads, ask yourself: Does this feel true to who I am? Does it align with my values? If you're not sure, that's okay—just pause and take a moment to get centered. Life will always throw things your way that pull you off track, but it's all part of the process. Just take a breath, check in with yourself, and gently get back on course.

Honoring Your Journey Without Judgment

One of the toughest things in life is not being hard on yourself, especially when things don't go as planned. But here's the truth: your journey is exactly that—yours. It doesn't look like anyone else's, and that's what makes it so powerful. There's no timeline you have to meet, no checklist you need to complete. Just keep showing up, doing your best, and honoring where you are right now.

You're going to face ups and downs, smooth days and tough ones. That's part of the ride. And when things don't go as planned, give yourself grace. There's no need to judge or compare—each step, each moment, is teaching you something you need to know. It's all part of your growth.

Continuing the Path of Growth, Peace, and Purpose

Alignment is a journey that doesn't end. There's always room for growth, peace, and more clarity. With each step you take, you learn more about who you are and what you're meant to do. The beautiful thing about this path is that it's not about reaching some final destination—it's about the unfolding of who you're becoming along the way.

Even when challenges pop up, they're not there to stop you—they're there to help you grow and get even more in tune with your purpose. So keep walking, keep trusting, and keep showing up for yourself. As long as you stay true to who you are and remember your deeper purpose, you're exactly where you need to be.

A Sacred Prayer for Alignment

In this moment, I pause and breathe deeply,
Calling myself into alignment with my truest self.
I give thanks to the Divine for guiding me with infinite wisdom and love.

May clarity fill my thoughts,
So I may see the truth clearly,
And may strength steady my body,
Grounding me in this moment, unwavering in the face of all that life presents.

May balance flow through my spirit,
Allowing me to walk with peace and purpose.
I am grateful for the lessons,
For the light and the shadows,
For each step of this journey that leads me toward deeper understanding.

Thank you for the ability to trust in the unfolding,
Knowing that all is happening as it should.
May I remain open, present, and true to the wisdom within me,
Letting my inner light shine brightly, reflecting the Divine's grace.

I walk forward with trust, peace, and gratitude, aligned with the flow of life.
May I stay rooted in balance, grounded in my essence,
And in harmony with the greater plan,
With every breath, every step, and every thought.

Thank you, Divine Presence, for always guiding me,
For always being with me,
And for the gift of alignment that continues to unfold.
So it is, and so it shall be.

ALIGNED

www.ingramcontent.com/pod-product-compliance
Lightning Source LLC
Chambersburg PA
CBHW050249010526
44107CB00003B/255